Author: Stuart Owen
Design: Druck Media Pvt. Ltd.
Publisher: Steve O'Hara
Published by: Mortons Media Group Ltd, Media Centre, Morton Way, Horncastle, Lincolnshire LN9 6JR
Tel. 01507 529529
Printed by: William Gibbons and Sons, Wolverhampton

ISBN: 978-1-911639-97-8

© 2022 **Mortons Media Group Ltd.** All rights reserved. No part of this publication may be reproduced or transmitted in any form or by any means, electronic or mechanical, including photocopying, recording, or any information storage retrieval system without prior permission in writing from the publisher.

Introduc

Quadrophenia and the mod revival helped to get the 1980s scooter scene off on a strong footing, with owners spread across the entire UK. Fashion was changing at a rapid pace and it wasn't long before the mod scene began to fizzle out – but the scooter owners remained. The parkas and smart suits were swapped for flight jackets and military-themed attire as a new revolution was born, the age of the scooter boys. With rallies building up a head of steam and as the decade progressed these would arguably be their greatest years.

Rallies were dotted around the country as thousands of scooterists flocked to seaside resorts on bank holidays and summer weekends. Unfortunately, so did others intent on causing trouble – trying to re-enact the old mods and rockers brawls of the 1960s. The media saw it as a quick buck, sensationalising and regurgitating fading stories from the past. While it didn't wash with those involved, it created havoc with local councils and residents who saw the typecast youth of the scooter scene as a threat. Regardless of all the court and legal issues the organisers just got on with it as the rallies got bigger and bigger.

Pride in a scooter's appearance had always been present but the individualism went up a notch as the custom scooter took a firm grip. Now only the best paint, chrome, and engraving would do as scooters outdid any other type of machine. As the competition became more competitive and intense so too did the creations with different styles appearing on an almost weekly basis. Full-bodied, cutdowns, choppers you name it, all being developed to the highest standards by the creative minds of those who owned them.

Midway through the decade, the entrepreneurs moved in – organising bigger and supposedly better rallies than ever before. Commercialisation meant changes and it was beginning to show an ugly side which many scooterists began to turn their backs on. The rallies would survive because the attendance was still big enough but diversity by way of other events catered for those who needed something different. As the sun began to set on the 1980s it was time to take a breath and reflect on what had been the biggest decade ever within the scooter scene. Most would carry on but it would never be the same as those involved had grown older and wiser, survivors of what had happened during those ten turbulent years.

PICTURE CREDITS AND THANKS

Wally Aylott, Tom Brown, Colin Cheetham, Steven Collins, Thomas Crinigan, Paul D'Arcy, Richard Dawson (RIP), Rob Dowding, Robert Doz Doyle, Simon Farrell, Steve Foster, Howard Gibson, John Gregory, Greg Harman, Dawn Lee, Adam Lyons, Alan Masterson, Paul Meeking, Paul Morton, Steve Moss, Frank Osgerby, Rich Oswald, Mark Sargeant, Gloria Saunders, Jamie Smith, Sean Wooden and the team at Mortons Archive

With the mod revival in full flow, seaside destinations became sought-after venues

Up north the invasion of towns reached epic proportions

ROADRUNNER SCOOTER CLUB 1980 OXFORDSHIRE

Open-face helmets and parkas became standard scooter riding equipment

No pub car park was safe any more

The Vespa PX would become the vanguard of Piaggio's attempt to take over the motorcycle world

Those early summers of the decade had no rules when it came to scooter fashion

Teenagers were ready to join the ranks of the scooter racing veterans of the 1970s

Patriotism – Lambretta style

A tired rider pauses while trying to do the impossible on a Vespa: the Paris-Dakar rally

BedIam
SCOOTERS
7 MILL STREET, BEDFORD

Try our

Lambretta
PHONE-A-PART-SERVICE

Phone BEDFORD (0234) 741309
9am - 9pm   7 days a week
or send for our free parts and accessory lists

The Old Bill, always waiting to strike once scooterists were in town

Grandma thinks the engine really has been stolen

He may have made himself famous on the track but now and then Dave Webster found time to go on scooter rallies, Scarborough '81

SCOOTERMANIA

ISSUE No: 1.

THE MAGAZINE FOR MOD/SCOOTERISTS NATIONWIDE

40p

The influence of The Jam was still huge, even though scooter fashions were changing at a rapid pace

Fifty held as scooter yobs riot

MODS went on the rampage as a scooter rally at the seaside turned to terror.

One of the main catalysts of the custom scooter in the 1980s, Clockwork Orange

Scooters and their owners barricaded B&Bs across the nation

The Luton and transit van, standard scooter club equipment by the 1980s

BRIGHTON SCOOTER RALLY 1982

at

BLACK ROCK CAR PARK
MADIERA DRIVE

Parking for 17th/18th July **£1**

Chrome doesn't get you home, but it does get you in a tape cassette advert

Carnaby Street may haave been the epicentre of fashion in the 1960s but two decades later it had become far too commercialised

Some of the modifications appearing on custom scooters didn't quite make sense

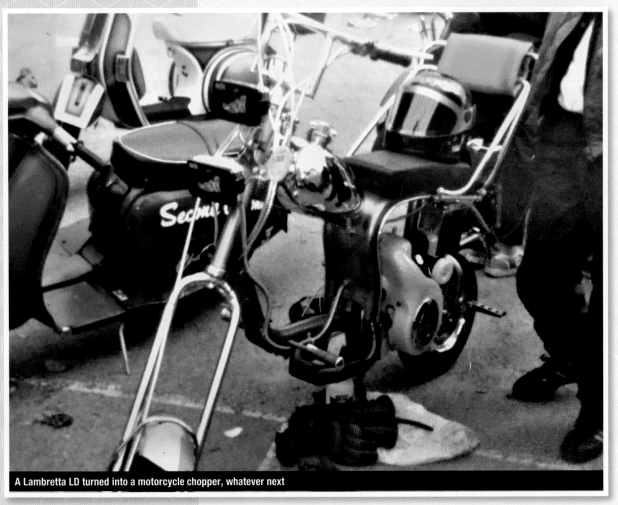

A Lambretta LD turned into a motorcycle chopper, whatever next

Perhaps a metal flake and chrome Vega

The J range – not always a favourite with the public but trying to gain acceptance

Frank Osgerby waiting to go out on track unfazed by the bigger competition

SUNDERLAND SCOOTER CLUB ARE
HOLDING A PARTY ON
FRIDAY 26th JUNE 1981
7.30 p.m. till 12.30 a.m.
TICKETS 50p

All Welcome: for details ring STEVE on
494759 or MICK on 490337 after 6 p.m

A young Rob Dowding is ready to become one of the scooter scene's newest recruits

Rightly so as on some occasions he would beat them at their own game

SCOOTER RIDERS STREAM INTO TOWN

WITH the arrival last night and this morning of the first influx of the expected 3,000 young scooterists from all parts of the country to invade Weymouth for their May Day weekend National Rally, extra police were drafted from other parts of Dorset to deal with any

For ladies as well, showing scooter riding belonged to everyone

It did seem like scooterists were beginning to own the road

The more reliable and easier-to-purchase Vespa began to dominate

To be honest any make would do if you wanted to be part of the movement

N.S.D. MALVERN 81

RETAIN
THIS PORTION
FOR ENTRY
INTO
DISCO

NATIONAL SCOOTER DAY

SATURDAY, 12th SEPTEMBER, 1981
noon till midnight

ADMIT ONE

Non-transferable

THREE COUNTIES SHOWGROUND MALVERN

ADMIT ONE

Non-transferable

The Ford, Escort or otherwise was no match for the scooter

NEW

jet set

No: 1   1981

40p

THE OFFICIAL MAGAZINE OF

lambretta club GREAT BRITAIN

Unless it was the backup van of course

Still trying to welcome the world as mod fashion shops moved in, but perhaps it was a bit too late

No city centre would be without its mods

Or petrol station forecourt

****

LEN'S SCOOTERS

Leeds Road
Tel. (0274) 584869

Vespa + Lambretta
dealers

Spares, Repairs
and Accessories

Custom paintwork
our speciality

****

A bit of class coming into the mod scene, thanks Tony

By now though clothing fashions were changing to a more military style

As the rallies became bigger the officers of the law didn't know how to take it

Looking almost dummy-like as they tried to enforce the rules

While scooterists would simply mimic them

SCOOTER MOB GOES ON THE RAMPAGE

Rally sites became dry dust bowls most of the time during the summer months

Concrete car parks offering the only other real alternative

Resorts with concentrated areas of B&Bs became adorned with wall-to-wall scooters

Whereas some roads became almost blocked off

Beware, while posing for the camera, that the owner of that car you just cut up isn't about to thump you one

DYROSPEED Scooters

79/81 East Street, Leeds.
Telephone: 0532 34905

New G.P.'s, Jets & Li 150 Specials
Tuned and Customised to your own specification

Custom covered seats
Fibre Glass G.P. Panels
Chroming Arranged
Amal and Del'Orto carbs

Also ring for details of our new race developed expansion chamber.

Organised chaos that was a scooter rally site

The Lambretta Grand Prix became the perfect platform for any painter to showcase their talents

For the Vespa it was the bulging side panel that offered the best option for artists

No cutdown could be without its breeze block stand to keep it upright

CHISELSPEED TUNING

ALANDALE MOTORS, ABERFORD ROAD, BARWICK IN ELMET, LEEDS.
Tel~812581 ASK FOR MARTIN.

* **High comp heads £5·00**
* **Head Reprofiling £7·16**
* **Barrel Tuning £16·00**

Yamaha MX Conversion Complete
You supply barrel + head. £47·50

* **Welding service (M.I.G.+ Oxy)**
* **Reboring.** * **NGK Spark Plugs.**
* **Bearings, oilseals, gaskets etc.**

* **KH 400 + 175 Conversions**
* **Competition Exhausts**
* **Expansion Chambers**

Prices on application.

Delivery service at race meetings see Martin of Central S.C.

ANDY DEAN 2nd Overall at Lydden using our barrel + head assembly

CHISELSPEED PERFORMANCE EQUIPMENT

Fast postal service, callers welcome.

For the late arrivals just leaving school and entering the fading mod scene the Vespa was the ideal power machine

Learning his trade to become one of the top scooter restorers in the country, Disco Dez

Those blokes from MSC know a thing or two about Lambretta clutches

When they needed a break scooterists would park up just about anywhere for a quick rest

Finding it difficult to get in any sort of order when parking up

The trophy presentation at the LCGB was always impressive, the most coveted award the Barcelona sword

Good old TAT, one of the most influential custom scooters ever built

Parking at rally sites was slightly more cramped for scooters than it was for cars

The new speed king of the 1980s, John Scrutton

AUTO-CYCLE UNION

CERTIFICATE
OF
NATIONAL RECORD

THIS IS TO CERTIFY THAT J. Scrutton

IS THE HOLDER OF THE FOLLOWING NATIONAL RECORD(S)

Catagory A2   Solo Scooters

Flying Start . Quarter Mile.

250cc Lambretta

8.365 secs - 107.59 m.p.h.

MADE AT Elvington

ON   5th, October 1986

Secretary General   Chairman, Auto Cycle Union

DATE   7th, April 1987

One of Birmingham's finest about to embark on his scooter career

Just a few years later, his transition to the scootering elite completed

Come To Kickstart

STATION GARAGE
BURNT ASH HILL
LONDON
SE12
TEL: 01-857-4908
GP-SERVETTA. VESPA
MAIN AGENTS
SPARES POSTAL SERVICE
New & Used Scooters
For Sale
& Always Wanted
TRY US
SOUTH EAST LONDON
SCOOTER CENTRE

Ready for the Isle of Wight 1984 – as soon as the old man shifts his car out of the way that is

Dave Batty receiving the LCGB BSM award from Norrie Kerr while the two main protagonists of the rally era sit on either side; was the split already happening?

Most rally life was spent sitting around on the streets

Custom scooters were there to be ridden whatever the weather

The Rally 200 was the Italian job

— SCOOTERAMA —
459 / 463 WARWICK ROAD,
TYSELEY, BIRMINGHAM B11 2JP.
— TELEPHONE 707 3431 —
24 HOUR ANSWERING SERVICE

What's that stuck on the front of that Lambretta?

Maybe not the first but one of the best-engineered water-cooled Lambrettas

All neatly hidden away

It's hard to tell whether or not they thought they were having the piss taken out of them

For now it was just scooters, but in a few years reshaping the rally scene with the VFM

★★★★★★★★★★★★★★★★★★★★★★★★★★★★★★★★★★★★★★★

LAMBRETTA   VESPA

Mikeck.
▦ RACING.

'CARLISLE SCOOTER CENTER'
89 London Road, Carlisle, Cumbria.

• Manufacturers of 'MIKECK' exhaust systems • Hydraulic disc brake conversions • Motoplat ignition kits (race use only) • Barrel tuning and conversion kits • Rear set kits • Vespa crankshaft mod. to racing specification • Plastic fans.

- - -LAMBRETTA- - -

• Mikeck Lamsuki 185,200,225,230 • Mikeck Lamsaki 150, road or race tuned • Crank rebuilds all models • Frame and fork shortening • Lambretta gas shocks • Machining work undertaken • Complete engine preparation • Amal & Dellorto carbs • Lambretta hydraulic brake pipes • Gaskets,oil seals,cables bearings etc.

- - - VESPA- - -

• Polini,Autissa 50/90,125/200 • Vespa Hydraulic disc brakes • Amal & Dellorto carbs • Special seats,choice of colours with Mikeck emblem for Vespa & Lambretta • Sign writing • Full range Vespa & Lambretta spares • Chrome parts to order.
Can deliver to road race meetings, mail order welcome, open 7 days a week. Call or phone anytime, personal attention to all enquires.
Tel: 0228 - 36944

★★★★★★★★★★★★★★★★★★★★★★★★★★★★★★★★★★★★★★★

Lambretta club
GREAT BRITAIN

Presents

CUSTOM CLASSIC
Scooter Show

Plus

BEEDSPEED/ L.C.G.B.
Five-A-Side Competition
at the

MADELEY COURT LEISURE CENTRE
Court St. Madeley, Telford, Shropshire.

Sun. 19th May '85

12 noon — 6·oo p.m.

£1·50 (L.C.G.B. members £1)

Licensed Bar & Hot Food Available
Trade Stalls on Show
& Many Other Attractions

Further Details: 0952 - 593164

No chance of feet touching the floor, but this was a 1980s scooter – it didn't matter

While the rat style required you to have that serious look

The coal shed became the number one choice of scooter garage

No wonder car drivers were nervous at motorway stations when scooterists pulled up

It was never easy getting out of one of those seaside resorts

Getting ready to change the course of rallies at a number ones meeting

Thank God it didn't rain that weekend

Leaving the town in a cloud of two-stroke fumes, why were they ever banned?

Thinking how far it is back home after a long weekend

Deciding the future of scooter rallies on a blackboard, while the wise one at the front fears how much damage commercialising them will do

Meanwhile, Mr Starr packs the crowds in

ON THE RUN 86

MEMBERS NOTICE

THE MANOR SUITE, PORTHCAWL

Friday, 4th July 8.00 p.m. - 8.00 a.m.

SCOOTERISTS ALL-NITER

● Keith Minshull ● Jon Beggs ● Dave Reed ● Jon Buck ●
NORTHERN — 6 Ts — REGGAE — SKA

*Plus the Sounds of the Meteors
and King Kurt*

Saturday, 5th July Lunchtime 12.00 Midday - 3.00 pm

"THE NO.1 ON THE RUN SPINNERS

Members Admission £1.00 Pay on the Day

Evening 8.00 p.m. - 8.00 a.m.

THE ALL- ALL-NITER

In Two Rooms
PLUS NEW TO THE RUNS

FRENZY

On Stage 12.00 Midnight

Members Tickets £5.00 from Rally Site or Manor Suite Ticket O

TROTSKYS CUSTOM SPRAY SERVICE

UNIT 8, MERCLOUGH MILLS, OFF WAKEFIELD ROAD, SOWERBY BRIDGE, HALIFAX, W. YORKS.

Top Quality Murals, Candies, Flakes, Leafing Repairs, etc. Murals £40 each.

Full scooter any colours from £80.

No VAT, Fast Turnover.

For Quote Please Ring
Halifax (0422) 59482.

SCOOTERING

May/June 1985.

Number 1.

FIRST ISSUE!

Inside: Street Scooters, Racers, Customs,
New Vespa Road-Tested, Runs and News.

Custom Lambrettas

Happening on an almost weekly basis, some of the best scooters ever built

Maybe sticking together gave the Vespa more impact

Looks a little on the bulky side compared to the Lambretta

The GP could be turned into a stunning custom scooter

So too the earlier models such as the Series 1

Then it changed in an instant, forever

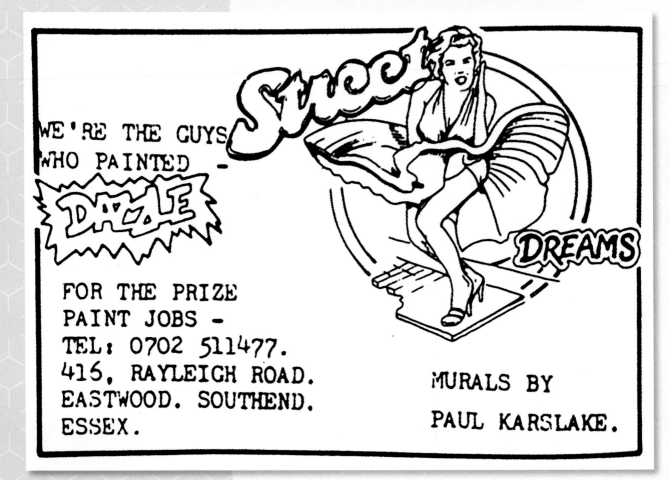

WE'RE THE GUYS WHO PAINTED — *Street*

DAZZLE

FOR THE PRIZE
PAINT JOBS —
TEL: 0702 511477.
416, RAYLEIGH ROAD.
EASTWOOD. SOUTHEND.
ESSEX.

DREAMS

MURALS BY
PAUL KARSLAKE.

Rainy daze

Innocenti could never have imagined anything like this could be done with the Lambretta

Lambretta club
GREAT BRITAIN
presents
A
CUSTOM / CLASSIC
SCOOTER SHOW
(more details overleaf)

AT THE
MADELEY COURT LEISURE CENTRE, COURT STREET,
TELFORD SHROPSHIRE

ADMISSION £1.50 — *£1 to L.C.G.B. Members*

SUNDAY 19th MAY 1985

12 noon to 6 p.m.

plus
BEEDSPEED SCOOTERS / L.C.G.B.

5 – A – SIDE FOOTBALL

"INTER SCOOTER CLUB EVENT"

1 -.m. to 5 p.m.

"ONLY 16 TEAMS" SO THE "1st TO PLAY" – £1 PER PLAYER

"TROPHIES TO ALL WINNING TEAM PLAYERS"

P. ORDER MADE PAYABLE TO "LCGB 5 A SIDE"

FURTHER DETAILS / ENTRY FORM FROM
R. DAWSON, 6 SPENCER, STANTONBURY 2, MILTON KEYNES, BUCKS
MK14 6BQ
TELEPHONE: 051-4269839

*   HOT FOOD   *   POOL TABLE   *   RECORD STALL   *

*   LICENSED BAR (12 to 6)   *   PATCH STALL   *   POSSIBLE FILM SHOW   *

ENTRIES TO BE IN BY MAY 1st ACCOMPANIED BY CHEQUE

JUNE 8TH & 9TH
Gates open mid day Friday 7th June

THE DONINGTON 2-DAYER

scooter

EVENT OF THE YEAR · SPONSORED BY VESPA UK...

DISC 85

DONINGTON INTERNATIONAL SCOOTER CLASSIC JUNE 8TH & 9TH

- ✦ **BAD MANNERS**
- ✦ **THE METEORS**
- ✦ **THE GENTS**
- ✦ **GYMKHANA**
  ENTRIES FREE ON THE DAY
- ✦ **TWISTY SPRINT RACING**
- ✦ **CUSTOM SHOW**
- ✦ **SCOOTER RACING**
- ✦ **VINTAGE SCOOTER SHOW**
- ✦ **EVENT PATCHES, BADGES, ETC.**
- ✦ **FREE PRESENTATION PACK ON ARRIVAL**
- ✦ **GIFT VOUCHER**
- ✦ **TRADE STANDS**
- ✦ **LICENSED BARS**
- ✦ **HOT FOOD AVAILABLE**

- ✦ **DJs**
- ✦ **TONY CLASS**
- ✦ **JOHN BUCK**
- ✦ **BILL BAKER**
- ✦ **DAVE REED**
- ✦ **BILL HOCKADAY**
- ✦ **NEIL RUSHTON**
- ✦ **CLUB STANDS**
- ✦ **FREE VESPA P 125ETS PRIZE DRAW**
- ✦ **ON SITE CAMPING**
- ✦ **WET T-SHIRT COMPETITION AND MUCH MORE, ETC.**
- ✦ **PRICE £5 – PAY ON ARRIVAL**

Scooters racing at one of the UK's premier tracks?

You bet they are

Sarge contemplating a move to Moto GP in the future

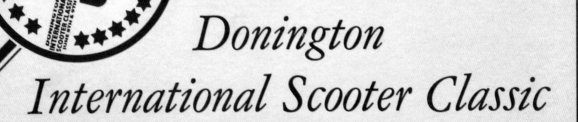

Donington
International Scooter Classic

8th & 9th June 1985
Competitors Certificate

This is to certify that

MARK SARGEANT

competed in the above event
organised by Vespa (UK) Ltd

Signed *Graham F George*

Sales Manager

Taking the Lambretta to a new height with extra wheels

Choppers became more and more insane

Stretching both the length and the imagination

Scooter racing getting more and more popular by the day with grids as long as your arm

SCOOTER AND SCOOTERIST

LAMBRETTA TUNING MANUAL

BY DAVE WEBSTER

UNDOUBTEDLY THE BEST TUNING WORK
EVER WRITTEN FOR THE LAMBRETTA.
SCOOTER ......FACTS, FIGURES ......

A WEALTH OF INFORMATION

Tuning technology was advancing rapidly but porting a cast barrel could take weeks to get it perfect

The hairpin at Cadwell Park was difficult to negotiate, more so in the wet as number 30 was about to find out

An engine and a half

Sometimes a gentle push is required to get a stubborn race Lambretta to fire up

E. M. S. A.
THREE SISTERS
PADDOCK PASS

date: comp./official

for conditions of admission see over

Group 6, where the rules were stretched that little bit further

Vespa T5
The 1986
Scooter sensation

PIAGGIO

As the decade wore on rallies became more established and overcrowded

Rally control LCGB style

Cold, wet, and dreary – no better
place for a rally to be held

It will never catch on

Taking a one-handed approach

THE NEW D.T.C.

SCOOTER CENTRE.

The one stop Custom shop

Everything from Performance Kits, Engraving, Chroming and Paintwork.

★ Lambretta Agent ★

New and Quality used Machines.

★ Half price Road ★ Race Paint On any New Machine Bought from Us

7, LOW ROAD, HUNSLET, LEEDS LS10 L80
TEL 0532 702728.

Dead level

Cool scooters deserve an audience

Projecting an image, number seven

Adam taking scootering seriously

If looks could kill

While Tom was just content at being a Lambretta owner

Custom shows were a day-long affair, so best to get comfortable

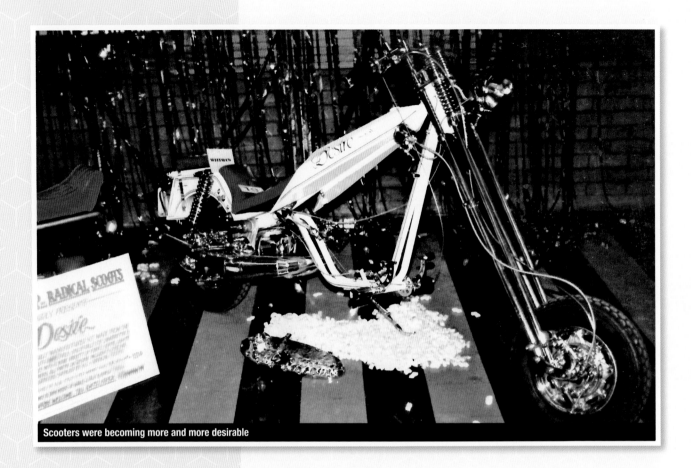

Scooters were becoming more and more desirable

Concerns were raised that scooters were changing beyond recognition

Thankfully there were still signs that they would remain within the boundaries of acceptance

Three wise men judging the best there was

All boxed up

The best scooters came from Sheffield

100mph on a Lambretta, why not

The show's over

Real scooter shops had everything an owner could want

Honda riders could only look on in envy at what they were missing out on

Mike receives the keys to another piece for his museum

Ray Kemp was determined to keep the Lambretta name alive

Always make sure your luggage is securely strapped down before setting off

Petrol station photos were standard practice, but you just wanted to get home

Posing by the destination signpost was a must on the way to a rally

The bigger the rally the bigger the clean-up operation afterwards

Mr Oswald entered into his third decade of scootering with a different machine, stolen but thankfully returned – allowing him to carry on his journey

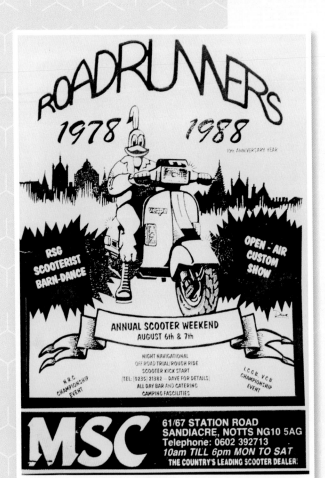

Yorkshire's finest

What a line-up

Fitting a Lambretta clutch is so easy you can do it blindfold

Chroming your scooter in the 1980s, this man would do it for you

Keeping the family tradition alive

The scooterist's workshop of the 1980s

It's easy to see where the street racer developed from

As scooters went faster it was obvious motorcycles would influence the designs

Classic lines led to classic designs

Dave's road-going Lambretta was full of performance-related ideas

The beginning of a new breed

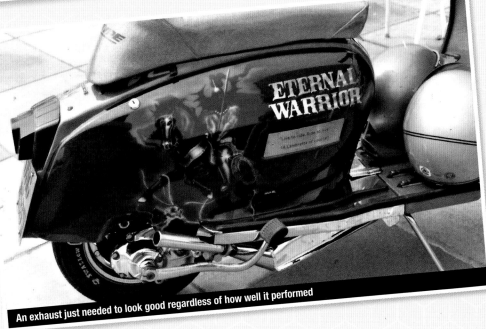

An exhaust just needed to look good regardless of how well it performed

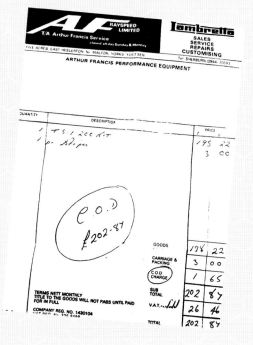

The original TS1 crew

Tom's Lambretta was soon converted to the new cylinder revolution

NATIONAL RUNS
COMMITTEE

1987
CLUB
MEMBER

No. C4 - 28

When health and safety was a less complicated affair

In the suburbs of Milan Lambretta history was being rediscovered

Laying idle at the back of a workshop, the rarest Lambretta in the world

Mike and Bob still making scootering history together

RedLam SCOOTERS

IT'S BACK THE NEW IMPROVED
SERVETA LYNX

ITALIAN STYLING WITH EUROPEAN QUALITY AND RELIABILITY
Just look at this STANDARD Specification!
AUTISA CYLINDER ASSEMBLY
POWERFUL NEW 12v LIGHTING SYSTEM – all 'E' marked – the first
'Lambretta style' machine to meet European lighting regulations.
12v AC Electrics with near flush body mounted indicators.
FRONT DAMPERS – Fitted as standard even on 125cc models.
LOCKABLE LEGSHIELD GLOVEBOX

125cc – £1150, 200cc – £1250 (ON THE ROAD PRICES)

Send large S.A.E for our new computerised price lists (state Vespa or Lambretta)
Visit our new showroom. Elstow Storage Depot is at Kempston Hardwick on the A421/B530
(previously A418) road between Bedford and Ampthill but remember we are closed on
Sundays and Mondays.

RedLam SCOOTERS

10C7A Elstow Storage Depot, Bedford MK45 3NU
Phone Bedford (0234) 741642. Open Tuesday—Saturday 9.30-5.30pm
After hours Phone Bedford (0234) 741309 or (0767) 60554 up till 8pm, 7 days a week

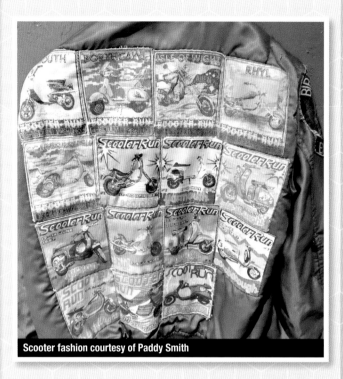

Scooter fashion courtesy of Paddy Smith

Going back to where we first started became the new idea

Designed in the 1960s and perfected in the 1980s

lambrettaclub

membership certificate

Trying to understand that it was once a Lambretta LD

Mr Cook conjuring up new designs all the time

A.F. Rayspeed Ltd. Catalogue

			PRICE	POST
AFS/01	Large Bore 42mm Silencer System Complete, up to 200cc [Pattern]		40.00	3.00
AFS/02	Large Bore 42mm Silencer System Complete, up to 200cc [Genuine]		52.00	3.00
AFS/03	Large Bore 48mm Silencer System Complete, for 225/250 [Pattern]		43.00	3.00
AFS/04	Large Bore Silencer System Complete 48mm, for 225/250 [Genuine]		55.00	3.00
AFS/05	Reverse Cone road Silencer with VW chrome pipe,42mm complete[Genuine]		67.00	3.00
AFS/06	Reverse Cone road Silencer with VW chrome pipe,42mm complete[Pattern]		57.00	3.00
AFS/07	Reverse Cone road Silencer with VW pipe[CHROME] 48mm complete. [Genuine]		70.00	3.00
AFS/08	Reverse Cone road Silencer with VW chrome pipe 48mm complete. [Pattern]		59.00	3.00
AFS/09	Fresco reverse Cone A.F. Expansion System,complete.42mm.		62.00	3.00
AFS/10	Fresco reverse Cone A.F. Expansion System,complete,in CHROME.42mm.		82.00	3.00
AFS/11	Fresco reverse Cone A.F. Expansion System,complete.48mm.		65.00	3.00
AFS/12	Fresco reverse Cone A.F. Expansion System,complete.48mm. CHROME.		86.00	3.00
AFS/13	Fresco Clubman Expansion system complete.42mm.		49.00	3.00
AFS/14	Fresco Clubman Expansion system complete.48mm.		52.00	3.00
AFS/15	Replacement 'U' bend for 42mm silencer system. flange not welded.		12.00	1.60
AFS/16	Replacement 'U' bend for 48mm silencer system. flange not welded.		14.00	1.60

LARGE BORE CLUBMAN   REVERSE CONE   FRESCO REVERSE CONE

AFS/17	Ancillotti slope back seat, various colours and two-tone.		34.95	3.50
AFS/18	Ancillotti square back seat, various colours and two-tone.		34.95	3.50
AFS/19	Snetterton seats, various colours and two-tone.		25.95	3.00
AFS/20	Metalflake seats; red,gold,brown,green,blue.SLOPE BACK,SQUARE BACK, SILVER,SILVER & BLACK.		38.95	3.50
	SNETTERTON.		29.95	3.00
AFS/20a	King and Queen seats, various colours.		36.95	3.50

SQUARE BACK   SNETTERTON   SLOPED BACK

AF TYPE

AFS/21	New Italian 200cc barrels.		27.50	2.90
AFS/22	New Italian 200cc barrels, complete with piston.		37.95	3.00
AFS/23	New Italian 200cc barrels, complete with piston and head.		47.95	3.25
AFS/24	New Italian 200cc barrel complete with Dykes piston,head,all stage 4.		72.98	3.25
AFS/25	Cylinder heads 125,150,175,200. state size.		10.50	1.75
AFS/26	Skimmed cylinder heads from 125 - 250cc. state size.		16.50	1.75
AFS/27	125cc barrel+piston.suit Li,Sx,Gp range.		41.90	3.00
AFS/28	125cc barrel, piston+head.		49.95	3.25
AFS/29	125cc barrel,piston+head.All stage 4 Tuned.		79.00	3.25
AFS/30	New Italian barrel.[225cc].		28.70	2.90
AFS/31	New Italian 225cc complete with piston.		45.95	3.00
AFS/32	New Italian 225cc barrel,piston,head.		55.40	3.25
AFS/33	New Italian 225 barrel,performance piston,head,all stage 4 tuned.		76.98	3.25
AFS/34	Amal mk2 30mm power jet carb,with manifold. state cc.		68.95	1.75
AFS/35	Amal mk2 34mm power jet carb,with manifold. state cc.		68.95	1.75
AFS/36	Amal mk2 30mm power jet carb,chrome slide+manifold. state cc.		74.80	1.75
AFS/37	Amal mk2 34mm power jet carb,chrome slide+manifold. state cc.		74.80	1.75
AFS/38	Amal mk2 manifold 30mm or 34mm. state size.		9.85	.75
AFS/39	Power jet kits for Amal mk2 carbs.state cc. L or R hand adjustment.		12.85	.50
AFS/40	Dellorto 30mm PHBH carb and manifold. sate cc.		41.75	1.75

FOR NON POWER JET CARBS PLEASE DEDUCT £7.00.

Champions on track and in the high street

Scooter shops before the internet age

MSC

61/67 STATION ROAD
SANDIACRE, NOTTS NG10 5AG
Telephone: 0602 392713
10am TILL 6pm MON TO SAT
THE COUNTRY'S LEADING SCOOTER DEALER!

No. 1 OUTRIGHT BRITISH SCOOTER CHAMPIONS 1983 '84, '85, '86 AND 1987

The shelves are brimming over with scooter spares – we stock all the parts that are available to us. We stock all the parts for current models and older models too, the list is endless. We export parts to most countries of the world . . . such is the demand!

New machines galore – Lambrettas are also stocked, but due to demand are rarely on display. If you want something special, contact MSC. We can supply everything you need – tuning, chroming, stove enamelling, engraving, etc etc. Trade-ins welcome, HP cleared, etc.

With over £200,000 worth of stock, MSC is your first stop for those parts you find difficult to obtain. We specialise in stocking scooter spares, be they big or small, slow fast moving . . try us first, we're here to help!

Huge stocks of chrome are at a premium at MSC. We offer an exchange service (if parts are suitable), and fully guarantee all our chrome. Quality is our 'byword', and it is evident by the standards of our chrome!

A 40 foot glass display counter keeps customers happy for hours, scanning the displays. The visual displays at MSC are a feature to behold. Every space has something to feast your eyes on . . . and it's all scooters . . . come on in and see!

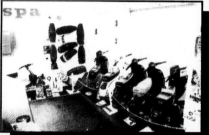

New and used machines are always at a premium at MSC. From the super T5 to the small PK50XL, we carry a full range of all Vespa scooters in a wide range of colours. We can prepare 'YOUR' Special, and do it just the way 'YOU' want it. Contact us for details.

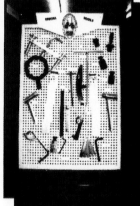

'Special tools' are another Midland Scooter Centre speciality. If they are available, we stock them – if not, we make them. We try to stock for all makes, Vespa and Lambretta. Ask for details.

Our tuning is **'Second to None'**, look at the results for the past 5 years, outright champions every time, remember that when you consider tuning for both Vespa and Lambretta, we lead the field with technology in Jap conversions, liquid cooling, reed valves, expansions, tuning etc. See us for details of our new Lambretta 200 Honda conversions.

MSC stock a full range of aftermarket expansion chambers. Simonini (Italy's Best), Pinasco, Shaft, Proma, Gianelli, Fresco, and of course the famous DJ system for Lambretta's and the Norrie Kerr system for Vespa PX/PE/T5's, all available in chrome or black

Midland Scooter Centre

Huge premises, vast stocks, expert staff. Dave Webster – Lambretta. Norrie Kerr – Vespa, Malc Anderson – Lambretta, Rob Kerr – Vespa. Janet Kerr - Secretary. Ellis Bednall - Despatcher. We're all here to help you.
Midland Scooter Centre - putting more back into scootering. In 1988 we're GIVING away 2 scooters and supplying thousands of pounds in

The Vespa PX was modern looking, but the owners created a custom style that transformed it

What are we waiting for?

"Can I feature that one in the magazine?"

Next stop, the other end of the country

Only 900 miles to the finish line

Keeping the LCGB flag flying high

N.R.C.

Trade and Custom Show

SATURDAY 29th OCTOBER 1988

AT

THE MANSFIELD LEISURE CENTRE
12 MIDDAY – 6pm

COMPLIMENTARY

Rather a strange location to unite the Lambretta world

Jim Trewin preparing to navigate the car park course as soon as Tino Sacchi gives the nod

Trade stalls were becoming part of custom shows to keep the format going

Mark Haines had a great understanding of what the scooterist needed and made a successful business from it

Kev hoping the wheels would
keep turning

Lambretta

PRESERVATION SOCIETY

Hon. Patron: P. J. AGS, Esq.

President: M. HOWARD KARSLAKE, FRSA, FInstB,

'KESTERFIELD' NORTHLEW,

NR. OKEHAMPTON, DEVON

The Society exists for all Enthusiasts of the
Lambretta, whether an Owner of a machine or not.

The prime object of its existence is the preservation of machines and artifacts, such as signs, badges,
photographs and publicity material, during the period of 1947 to 1971.

Machines to be included on the register must be renovated to original condition and as near to their
production specification as possible.

Rallies are organised in conjunction with the Lambretta Club of Great Britain, and information is
available on the various models, as well as advice on the renovation and restoration of machines.

The Society also gives the opportunity of past Owners and Club Members to keep in touch with
their previous contacts in the Lambretta sphere.

Twenty years after he had first seen it, Mike Karslake finally got to ride the Lambretta twin cylinder

The Cosa was designed to be the future for Piaggio, no thanks

The decade when scootering was still affordable

Ray Kemp was determined to bring the Lambretta into the 21st century

By the end of the decade the TS1 had taken over

Lambrettas could still be picked up for an affordable price

Shops were catering for those who wanted to restore them

And scootering's most famous son had achieved his dream